# RAND

# Russian National Security and Foreign Policy in Transition

*Eugene B. Rumer*

*Prepared for the*
*United States Air Force*

**Project AIR FORCE**

This report examines critical trends in and the evolution of Russian thinking on foreign and national security policy from near the end of the Gorbachev era to today's post–Soviet Russia. The report provides an assessment of these trends and their implications for U.S. interests and policy. It should be of interest to intelligence analysts and strategic planners concerned with developments in the former Soviet Union, Europe, and Asia.

This report was written as part of a project entitled "Moscow's Alternative Security, Foreign, and Economic Policies." It is based on extensive interviews with Soviet and Russian academics, journalists, military personnel, Foreign Ministry and other government officials, parliamentarians, and political activists, conducted in Moscow between 1989 and 1993. The report also draws on a review of publicly available Soviet and Russian publications. **Research for this report was completed in August 1994.**

The research was conducted under the auspices of the Strategy, Doctrine, and Force Structure program of Project AIR FORCE, at RAND.

## PROJECT AIR FORCE

Project AIR FORCE, a division of RAND, is the Air Force federally funded research and development center (FFRDC) for studies and analyses. It provides the Air Force with independent analyses of policy alternatives affecting the development, employment, combat readiness, and support of current and future aerospace forces.

Research is being performed in three programs: Strategy, Doctrine, and Force Structure; Force Modernization and Employment; and Resource Management and System Acquisition.

Project AIR FORCE is operated under Contract F49620-91-C-0003 between the Air Force and RAND.

# CONTENTS

Russian thinking on foreign and security policy is undergoing a fundamental transformation. The consensus of the Gorbachev and Yeltsin eras that had promised to launch the Soviet Union and Russia on the path of strategic rapprochement and even partnership with the Western alliance has been replaced by a new consensus. The new consensus puts far less emphasis on the maintenance of a cooperative partnership with the West and promises to push Russia toward a more aloof position relative to the Western alliance. This consensus is preoccupied with regions and countries along Russia's immediate periphery, is prone to outbursts of great-power assertiveness, and is seeking to rebuild Russia's sphere of influence. At best it is a consensus regarding Russia's special responsibility in the Commonwealth of Independent States (CIS). At worst it is a consensus about Russia's special right in the former Soviet Union as its presumed exclusive sphere of influence.

This direction in Russian foreign policy is the result of the domestic political and economic transformation of Russia in the first two years following the breakup of the Soviet Union. The shock of early post-Soviet reforms, which were closely identified with the pro-Western course of the Gaydar cabinet, has produced a significant degree of disillusionment with the West and the United States, as well as with the course of a close partnership with Washington. The depth of Russia's economic decline and the long road to recovery would, in the eyes of many Russians, effectively preclude Moscow's participation in that partnership as an equal. Hence, Russia needs to pursue its own independent course in foreign and security policy commensurate with its means and consistent with its great-power aspirations.   The gradual replacement of Western-oriented "market romantics" in Moscow's policymaking arena with "pragmatists" who identify more closely with large state interests has been accompanied by a change in rhetoric that has come to emphasize closer relations with the post-Soviet states, the "near abroad," as a key goal of Russian foreign policy.

Russia's military establishment, already marred by allegations of widespread meddling in various regional conflicts in the former Soviet Union, has embraced the notion that the "near abroad" will remain a sphere of vital interest and exclusive influence of Russia. The refocusing of the Russian military's attention on the "near abroad" has been amply demonstrated in the military doctrine adopted in 1993.

This picture of institutional consensus is complemented by the legislative branch—the Duma.  The presence of large statist—communist, agrarian, nationalist, and industrialist—interests virtually guarantees that the new legislature will not engage in aggressive pursuit of a pro-Western foreign and security policy course any more than the last one did, and that its efforts will be devoted to the task of defining and protecting Russian interests in the "near abroad." Pragmatism, realism, and gradualism have emerged as the key themes of the new Russian consensus in the areas of national security and foreign policy.  This consensus has often been narrowly interpreted as a sign of Russian self-interest.

Pragmatism in Russian foreign and security policy has also manifested itself in a greater appreciation of the likely implications of neoimperialist ambitions for the domestic economy and politics should the Russian government actively seek to establish an exclusive sphere of influence throughout the former Soviet Union.  Fiery rhetoric and Monroe-like doctrines expounded by Russian foreign policy ideologues have so far been left unmatched by concrete action when it comes to the practical details of closer association with neighbors whose economies show no sign of improvement. Even the most ardent neoimperialists pause at the thought of reintegration with Belarus or Ukraine.  Ideological neoimperialism and great-power ambition meet with economic reality that, to date, has served as an effective constraint on them.

The Russian quest for a lasting vision of national interest and a place in the international arena without the Soviet Union poses a number of difficult questions for U.S. policymakers, and the answers to them are likely to have far-reaching implications for U.S. post–cold war policy, not only toward the former Soviet Union but also toward other regions of the world.

A key issue in this context is the contradiction between U.S. recognition of sovereignty, independence, and territorial integrity of the newly independent states around Russia's periphery on the one hand, and Russian aspirations for a special role in the "post-Soviet space" on the other. U.S. interest in maintaining good relations with Russia could come into conflict with Russia's claim to a *droit de regard* over the newly independent states. In the view of this author, under the best of circumstances Russia could and should play the role of the pillar of security and stability in the former Soviet Union. Under a far less optimistic, and perhaps more realistic, scenario, Russian pursuit of national interest could impinge on its neighbors' sovereignty.

U.S. policymakers would face the task of balancing the newly independent states' right to sovereignty against the need to restore order in a given region, as well as against the desire to sustain continuity in U.S.-Russian relations. Recognizing the tension between the obligations of international law and the realistic limitations on U.S. foreign policy, one has little choice but to acknowledge that our commitment to furthering the principles of self-determination, sovereignty, and territorial integrity will have to be constrained by practical concerns for prevention of conflict and loss of life. In the view of this author, such considerations must take precedence over the principles of sovereignty and territorial integrity, as well as the desire for self-determination. Although little can be done after the fact, it is also important to recognize, with a view toward future contingencies, that in some instances recognition of the newly independent states in recent years may have been premature.

No easy solutions are available to Western and Russian policymakers to alleviate problems in the existing situation or to avert contingencies. Even formal recognition (however difficult it would prove to codify) of Russia's special role of oversight throughout the former Soviet Union still begs the question of Russia's ability to play that role. At the same time, it is important for the international community to recognize that Russia does play a special role in that sphere and it has special interests there. To deny this would be unrealistic, unfair, and unwise.

Admittedly, the Western community has little leverage over Russian policies, both real and declaratory, toward the former Soviet Union. But it can play a constructive role, albeit remaining on the periphery. Stabilization through economic assistance to the "lesser equals" in the CIS could prove beneficial to Russia's own interests. Perhaps, given Russia's uncertain stance in relation to its neighbors, the best that the West can do is to help create a more stable environment around it.

# INTRODUCTION

February 7, 1990, was a day of unprecedented change in the history of the Soviet Union. On that day the Communist Party (CPSU) leadership surrendered its constitutional monopoly on the country's political life and process by agreeing to amend Article VI of the Soviet Constitution, which had previously guaranteed it that right.

As often happened during the perestroyka years, that decision lagged behind the real course of political events in the Soviet Union and represented, as many measures taken by the Soviet leaders, a half step that left both opponents and proponents of reforms dissatisfied. But the importance of that highly symbolic step should not be underestimated. The CPSU, which for nearly three-quarters of the 20th century had enjoyed an absolute constitutional monopoly on ideas, had in effect sanctioned political competition and ideological challenge to its dogma. For the first time in Soviet history, citizens were allowed to form and join political parties other than the CPSU.

Following that constitutional change, dozens of new political parties and popular movements of every political persuasion and purpose have come out in the open, registered with the government, and stepped into the political arena. The parties and movements have ranged from the notorious, rabidly nationalist and xenophobic *Pamyat'* (which seeks to protect Russia from a conspiracy of Zionists and Freemasons) and the misnamed Liberal-Democratic Party (which advocates restoration of the Russian Empire to its pre-1917 boundaries) to the democratic and market-oriented Russian Republican Party and the Universalist Party (whose principal goals include abolition of the death penalty and protection of abortion rights).

This parade of political parties has had relatively little effect on turbulent Soviet and Russian domestic politics. In addition, not one political party has achieved national recognition at the grass-roots level. The reasons behind these particular occurrences are complex and lie outside the scope of this study. The abolition of Article VI of the old Soviet constitution was important not because newly founded political parties entered the domestic political process and made a difference. They did not. But the event marked the formal beginning of an open political discourse on a broad range of policy and political issues. It opened doors to competing visions of national interest, replacing the Communist Party's formal ideological monopoly with a free marketplace of ideas.

No debate in this marketplace has been more important for Russia, its immediate neighbors and former colonies, as well as the rest of the outside world, than the debate about national security and national interest. Deeply rooted in Russia's own domestic political and ideological transformation, the debate brought to the fore of the country's ideological agenda the centuries-old question of Russia's strategic orientation and relationship with the West, most importantly with the United States and Western Europe. Should Russia attempt to join the Western free-market democracies and, in the process, transform itself internally into a compatible partner with a market economy and a pluralistic political system, or should it maintain its distance from the West, seeking its own unique path of internal transformation?

It is only natural that foreign policy and national security would play a pivotal role in Russian internal debates about national interest. The country's domestic economic and political transformation could not begin without addressing national security and foreign policy questions first. The need to alleviate the crippling defense burden on the Soviet and Russian economy made it imperative that a different understanding of national security requirements and relations with the outside world be developed.

Debates about national security and foreign policy had preceded the abolition of Article VI of the Soviet Constitution. But the change made in February 1990 marked the turning point that, in effect, legalized open discourse about national interest and national security, and permitted its participants to articulate their views freely, without resorting to the Aesopian language of Soviet propaganda. That debate has continued to the present day, as Russia pursues its internal transformation and quest for a stable vision of national interest and national security.

Soviet and Russian debates about foreign policy and national security have followed the domestic political trends in the country. Most of the Gorbachev era was devoted to discussions of rapprochement with the West and clearing away the military and political baggage of the cold war to make that rapprochement possible. But as the central Soviet government lost its power and authority, and Russia began to emerge from the Soviet Union, the field of the discourse expanded to include Russian visions of national security and foreign policy, encompassing such issues as the fate of the Russian/Soviet empire and Russia's relations with other Soviet republics.

The demise of the Soviet Union refocused the debate on the subjects of Russian national security and Russian national interest. But the essence of the questions under consideration remained the same: relations with the West and the nation's immediate neighbors. Whereas during the Gorbachev era, Soviet relations with the West were often considered through the prism of Moscow's policies toward its Warsaw Pact vassals, Russia's international behavior has been judged in the West largely by its dealings with the former republics along its western border. The border has changed, but the issues have not.

Moscow's search for equilibrium in relations with its neighbors, whether they are termed the Warsaw Pact or the "near abroad," as well as with the more distant industrialized West, has continued since the breakup of the Soviet Union. Balance has yet to be found in many areas of Russian national security and foreign policy: between reexpansion and responsible behavior as a stabilizing regional actor, between cooperation with the West and subservience to it, and between integration into the community of industrialized democracies and the search for its own independent path of development.

This report provides an overview of the progression from Soviet to Russian debates about key aspects of national security and foreign policy relations with the United States and its West European allies, as well as with Russia's immediate neighbors in Eastern and Central Europe. It covers the period from near the end of the Gorbachev era to the present and examines the national security and foreign policy debate against the backdrop of key trends in Soviet and Russian domestic politics. The report concludes with policy implications for the United States.

# GLASNOST: DOMESTIC POLITICS AND FOREIGN POLICY

The monolith of Soviet official thinking and expression on foreign and security policy had cracked long before Article VI of the Soviet Constitution was abolished in February of 1990. The crack occurred as a deliberate element of a major domestic political battle fought by President Mikhail Gorbachev against the entrenched military interests that had traditionally dominated Soviet foreign and national security policy.

Revitalization of the stagnating Soviet economy was a key task facing the Gorbachev regime from its outset in 1985. However, as the regime's attempts to jump-start the economy proved unsuccessful, it became increasingly clear to a growing number of Gorbachev's advisors that no economic policy would be successful without a significant reduction in the crushing military burden.[1]

But that task could not be accomplished without two key conditions: an articulation of a radically different vision in the area of national security and an assault on the preponderant role of the military institution in the formulation of national security policy. A new national security policy could not be articulated by the ossified Soviet military institution. The source of new vision was found by Gorbachev in the civilian community of academics, who, until the late 1980s, had played a marginal role in Soviet national security deliberations, hav-

---

[1]Interviews with Soviet academics, Foreign Ministry officials, and Central Committee staffers, Moscow, December 1989 and February–March 1990. See also Henry S. Rowen and Charles Wolf, Jr., eds., *The Impoverished Superpower: Perestroyka and the Soviet Military Burden*, ICS Press, San Francisco, 1990.

ing been largely relegated to the task of putting the best face on Soviet policy before Western audiences.[2]

In the tradition of ambiguity of official Soviet statements, Gorbachev uttered the key words at the 27th Party Congress in 1986:

> Guaranteeing security appears more and more as a political prob-
> lem which can be solved only through political means.[3]

Gorbachev called for a significant revision of Soviet military doctrine and sanctioned more active civilian participation in the formulation of the defense policy. In what can be now considered as the key pro-nouncement on defense/foreign policy matters, the General Secretary declared that the Soviet quest for security had in the past relied too much on military means and failed to take full advantage of political instruments—a shortcoming that, he claimed, must be corrected.[4]

"Political means" were clearly a nonmilitary matter in the tradition of Soviet civil-military relations, the exclusive preserve of civilians. The change called for increased participation of the latter in the formula-tion and conduct of Soviet foreign and national security policy. Gorbachev challenged the country's national security establishment, which now included civilian analysts as well as the military, to fill with meaning his new doctrine of "reasonable sufficiency," which was to guide Soviet security policy. The race to fill the shell of "reasonable sufficiency" with meaning began between civilian pro-ponents of downsizing the Soviet military burden and military advo-cates of the status quo.

In addition to the intellectual assault on the military's monopoly on formulation of national security policy, the political leadership re-

---

[2]For a detailed treatment of this phenomenon, see Benjamin Lambeth, *Is Soviet Defense Policy Becoming Civilianized?* R-3939-USDP, RAND, 1990; John Van Oudenaren, *The Role of Shevardnadze and the Ministry of Foreign Affairs in the Making of Soviet Defense and Arms Control Policy*, R-3898-USDP, RAND, 1990; and A. Alexiev and R. Nurick, eds., *The Soviet Military Under Gorbachev: Report on a RAND Work-shop*, R-3907-RC, RAND, 1990.

[3]Mikhail Gorbachev, Speech at the XXVII Party Congress, Radio Liberty Monitoring Service, 2/25/86, p. 94 (11).

[4]Ibid.

sorted to a series of unprecedented steps designed to undermine the image of competence and infallibility of the military institution cultivated in the Soviet Union throughout its entire post–World War II history. An opportune moment to launch such an assault was presented in May of 1987 when a German teenager made a mockery of Soviet air defenses by landing a small aircraft just outside the Kremlin. The incident was followed by an unprecedented public condemnation of the country's military leadership for incompetence and an extensive purge in the upper echelons of the Ministry of Defense.[5] It served an important domestic political purpose: The military and its opinion in national security matters were now open to questioning from various quarters, from writers to civilian analysts in academic institutes.

The challenge to the military institution from the civilian community created two conflicting visions in the Soviet national security arena. The first—radical—vision, asserted by increasingly outspoken and influential civilian analysts, sought reconciliation, even alliance, with the West in general and the United States in particular. Such reconciliation was key to the success of Soviet domestic reforms, which required a reduction of the military burden and greater cooperation with the West as the source of much-needed investment and technology. The United States and NATO posed no military threat to Soviet security interests. Hence, the Soviet military presence in Europe could be reduced substantially, leading to significant reductions in the overall size of the military establishment; far-reaching military reform, including a transition to an all-volunteer force; and a fundamental shift in Soviet military strategy from an overall emphasis on offensive operations to a generally defensive posture designed to protect Soviet security interests against increasingly unlikely external aggression, but unsuitable for offensive operations.[6]

---

[5]*Krasnaya Zvezda*, May 31, 1987.

[6]Eugene B. Rumer, *The End of a Monolith: The Politics of Military Reform in the Soviet Armed Forces*, R-3993-USDP, RAND, 1990; V. Zhurkin, S. Karaganov, and A. Kortunov, "Reasonable Sufficiency—or How to Break the Vicious Circle," *New Times*, No. 40, 1987, p. 13; see also "O razumnoy dostatochnosti," *SShA*, No. 12, 1987, by the same authors; A. Kokoshin, and V. Larionov, "Kurskaya bitva v svete sovremennoy oboronitel'noy doktriny," *Mirovaya ekonomika i mezhdunarodnyye otnosheniya*, No. 8, 1987; A. Kokoshin, "A. A. Svechin. O voyne i politike," *Mezhdunarodnaya zhizn'*, No. 10, 1988; and S. Blagovolin, "Voyennaya moshch'—skol'ko, kakaya, zachem?" *Mirovaya ekonomika i mezhdunarodnyye otnosheniya*, No. 8, 1989.

The second vision—status quo—articulated with increasing assertiveness by the hard-line members of the military establishment,
was wedded to the old traditional concepts of military threat from
NATO and the United States, a strictly numerical understanding of
military balance and military strategy based on the principle that the
best defense is offense. The Soviet military, they claimed, did not
pose a threat to anyone; it was already being maintained within the
confines of reasonable sufficiency with no fat to trim. By contrast,
NATO and the United States, they argued, enjoyed significant advan-
tages in many areas of military technology and capabilities and
posed a significant challenge to Soviet security. The military establishment resisted discussions of military reform in the Soviet Armed
Forces and opposed cuts in the size of the military institution. The
much-publicized Soviet reduction of 500,000 troops in Eastern
Europe announced by Gorbachev in December of 1988 was publicly
resisted by then Chief of the General Staff Marshal Akhromeyev, as
well as other senior military officers.[7] Akhromeyev resigned from his
post soon after the announcement of unilateral cuts.

With the rapid acceleration of political changes in Eastern Europe
and the Soviet Union, the newly empowered community of civilian
analysts of military and foreign policy matters began to articulate a
much bolder vision for Soviet policy toward Europe and the United
States. Following the opening of the Berlin Wall, that vision included
abandonment of the concept of two German states and their unification with continuing participation in NATO; withdrawal of the
(increasingly tenuous and unwelcome) Soviet military presence in
Eastern Europe; and Soviet integration into the so-called "Common
European Home," in which a pivotal role would belong to the United
States as an important stabilizing factor, guarding against the specter
of German revanchism and providing a reassuring presence for the
Soviet Union and other European powers. The U.S. presence on the
continent was explicitly mentioned in the Soviet foreign policy and
national security community as one of the key factors safeguarding
European security and stability. The possibility of U.S. withdrawal
from Europe alarmed those Soviet analysts who feared the decline of

---

[7]"Reliable Defence First and Foremost," *Moscow News*, No. 8, 1988, p. 12; *Svenska Dagbladet*, November 30, 1988, p. 3; translated in FBIS-SOV-88-234, December 6, 1988, pp. 119–120.

Soviet military and economic strengths relative to those of the West and especially to those of Germany.[8]

Soviet military withdrawal from Eastern Europe and German unification were seen by many Soviet civilian analysts as a precondition for normalizing relations with countries in the region, which in turn would serve as Moscow's bridge to Europe and to the West in general. A unified and friendly Germany would, in their eyes, play the role of the key pillar in that alliance.[9]

Needless to say, that vision was not widely shared among the upper echelons of the Soviet military establishment. Steeped in the traditions, history, and military-theoretical heritage of World War II, the Soviet High Command found itself in opposition to the Gorbachev administration policies on Europe. German unification and withdrawal from Eastern Europe amounted to the abandonment of the entire European theater of military operations, which was built on a vast investment in infrastructure and concepts of military operations established over the course of nearly half a century.[10]

In addition to the loss of territory, infrastructure, and strategy resulting from the end of Soviet military occupation of Eastern Europe, the military also faced the daunting task of redeploying its Eastern European contingent back to the USSR. Ill-prepared for such massive dislocation, it found itself unable to cope with the challenge of redeploying and housing hundreds of thousands of troops, officers, and their families, thus adding to an already acute internal crisis in

---

[8]Interviews with academics and Foreign Ministry officials. Moscow, December 1989 and September–October 1990; Eugene B. Rumer, *The German Question in Moscow's "Common European Home": A Background to the Revolutions of 1989*, N-3220-USDP, RAND, 1991; R. G. Bogdanov, Speech at the MFA Conference, *Mezhdunarodnaya Zhizn'*, No. 10, 1988; *Vestnik Ministerstva Inostrannykh Del SSSR*, No. 15, 1988, p. 24; and "Glavnyy Protivnik—Inertsiya Gonki Vooruzheniy," *SShA: Ekonomika, Politika, Ideologiya*, No. 10, 1988.

[9]Sergei Blagovolin, "Warsaw Treaty Organization—Farewell to Arms," *Moscow News*, No. 9, 1991.

[10]See John Kohan, "It's Lonely up There," *Time*, July 16, 1990; "We Are Not Going to Surrender," *Krasnaya Zvezda*," June 21, 1990; "From the Position of Perestroyka," *Pravda*, June 20, 1990; V. Nadein, "What General Makashov's Statements Are Aimed at," *Izvestiya*, June 20, 1990; and "Viktor Alksnis Says USSR Has Betrayed Our Allies," *Kommersant*, March 18, 1991.

the military caused by deteriorating socioeconomic conditions in the officer corps.[11]

Despite the apparent resentment of these policies among the Soviet military establishment, there was relatively little overt criticism of them from the ranks of the uniformed officers.[12] The High Command found a surrogate voice in the increasingly outspoken conservative opposition, which was composed of new reactionary political parties and independent analysts.

The objections voiced by these analysts to the Gorbachev-Shevardnadze foreign and security policy fell largely along the lines of traditional Soviet fears of German revanchism and U.S. anti-Soviet aggression in Europe aimed at surrounding the Soviet Union with a belt of hostile states, as well as resentment of voluntary Soviet with-drawal from its sphere of influence in Eastern Europe.  In these ana-lysts' eyes, Soviet influence in Eastern Europe constituted one of the greatest accomplishments of the Soviet state and the fruits of Soviet victory in World War II.  Perceiving the West as inherently hostile to Russia and the Soviet Union, they often argued that the Gorbachev-Shevardnadze foreign policy was fundamentally harmful to Soviet and Russian interests as a great power.[13]

These views, expressed with increasing shrillness by the representa-tives of the extreme right wing of the Communist Party and a loose coalition of Russian nationalists, were nonetheless relegated to a mi-nority position.  The emerging consensus among the Soviet and Russian foreign policy establishment was decidedly pro-Western—a phenomenon that was documented not only through Soviet adher-ence to the general Gorbachev-Shevardnadze foreign policy line even after the latter's resignation in the winter of 1990, but through Soviet cooperation with, and support of, the allied coalition in the

---

[11]On this see Eugene B. Rumer, *The End of a Monolith:  The Politics of Military Reform in the Soviet Armed Forces*, R-3993-USDP, RAND, 1990.

[12]Among the few notable exceptions were USSR People's Deputies Alksnis and Petrushenko and the notoriously conservative editor of the *Military-Historical Journal*, General Viktor Filatov.  Their public outspokenness on issues of foreign and security policy was not typical of the Soviet officer corps at large.  The majority of the officer corps evidently had preferred that the "military be kept out of politics."

[13]Interview with Aleksandr Prokhanov, Viktor Alksnis, Viktor Filatov, and Vladimir Zhirinovskiy, Moscow, September–October 1990 and February–March, 1991.

Gulf War (which undermined the previously close Soviet-Iraqi relationship).

The strength of that consensus and the seemingly permanent nature of the radical shift in Soviet foreign and security policy were reflected in the fact that the Gorbachev-Shevardnadze foreign and security policies had received virtually unqualified support from the overwhelming majority of new democratically oriented political parties and, most importantly, even from Gorbachev's most powerful source of domestic opposition—the "Democratic Russia" movement—led by Russian President Boris Yeltsin.[14]

Although engaged in a fierce domestic political struggle with Gorbachev, Boris Yeltsin and his pro-reform coalition had endorsed the foreign policy of the Gorbachev administration. Furthermore, on a number of national security issues, such as military reform, Yeltsin and his supporters had staked out a more progressive agenda than Gorbachev's. During the latter's temporary alliance with the coalition of Soviet hard-liners in the winter of 1990–91, the apparent strength of Yeltsin and his supporters in the domestic political arena was perceived by many students of Soviet politics as a powerful impediment to a potential reversal in Soviet security policy.

Moreover, in a peculiar twist, many of Gorbachev's former advisors from the circle of civilian security specialists who had played an important role in formulating his foreign and security policies had, by the winter of 1990–91, unequivocally joined, or established good ties with, the Yeltsin camp. Their ranks included such prominent Soviet academic specialists as former Chairman of the Foreign Affairs Committee of the Supreme Soviet Yevgeniy Ambartsumov, Deputy Defense Minister Andrey Kokoshin, Director of the USA and Canada Institute Georgiy Arbatov, and academicians Oleg Bogomolov and Yuriy Ryzhov, among others. These moves had all but assured a high degree of intellectual continuity between the foreign and security policies of the Gorbachev administration and Yeltsin's.

There were several other factors that accounted for that high degree of continuity and pro-Western orientation of the future Yeltsin government of independent Russia. First among these was the per-

---

[14]Interview with Russian Foreign Minister Andrey Kozyrev, March 1991.

ceived value of external support for domestic political, economic, and societal reforms espoused by Russia's democratic movement. Many of its members believed, at the time, that the weight of Western public opinion was the only thing that stood between them and the threat of a reactionary crackdown to which, they feared, Gorbachev would acquiesce.[15]

The second factor—also from the realm of Russian domestic politics—was Yeltsin's ideological and political program. That program openly called for dismantling the Soviet empire and transforming it into a union of equal partners linked by a new federal treaty or a series of bilateral treaties.

The domestic political purpose of that program was apparent: to undermine the influence of the union center and Gorbachev personally. But the rhetoric that was used to articulate the program emphasized the importance of dissolution of the internal empire and was therefore fully consistent with, and in effect directly followed from, the goal of the Gorbachev-Shevardnadze foreign policy aimed at dismantling the external empire. In fact, nothing short of a full and aggressive pursuit of the Gorbachev-Shevardnadze foreign policy could have been consistent with the domestic agenda of the Yeltsin coalition.

Finally, the general goal of democratic and free-market reform espoused by the Yeltsin coalition was, in the view of many of its key members, unattainable without extensive ties to and support from the West, in particular the United States. Many, among them prominent civilian analysts who had played an important role in the formulation of the Gorbachev-Shevardnadze foreign policy strategy, shared the view of prominent academic and political activist Yevgeniy Ambartsumov, who was to become Chairman of the Foreign Affairs Committee of the Russian Supreme Soviet. He wrote at the end of 1989:

---

[15]Interviews, Moscow, February–March 1991.

> I am convinced that the world community is . . . interested in over-
> coming our crisis.[16]

Yeltsin's domestic program was popularly dubbed "Little Russia," to reflect its key idea—the need for Russia to abandon its imperial baggage and devote its energies to the task of internal reconstitution. In addition to the support it received from the umbrella coalition of the new democratic parties and informal movements, as well as the circle of liberal intelligentsia that had previously supported Gorbachev's innovative domestic and foreign policies, "Little Russia" gathered considerable popular support in the course of two national elections—for the Supreme Soviet of the Russian Federation in 1990 and for the Presidency of Russia in 1991.

Both elections, but especially the 1991 presidential election, demonstrated the strength of grass-roots support for the concept of "Little Russia," on which Boris Yeltsin and the democratic slate had founded their platform. That support was particularly striking when compared with the poor showing of the reactionary coalition in both elections. Its candidates, highly critical of the Gorbachev-Shevardnadze foreign and national security policies, argued that Soviet and Russian national interest required that these policies be reversed, that the military institution be strengthened and take the key role in the conduct of domestic and foreign policy, and that the Soviet defense-industrial sector serve as the basis for the rejuvenation of Russia's economy. They also demanded that the weakened union government be restored, if necessary by force, to its pre-perestroyka position of unchallenged power and authority. Moscow, they argued, had no alternative but to return to great-power, imperial policies throughout its internal and external empires.[17]

These candidates and their views did poorly in the elections. Their xenophobic, anti-Western, chauvinistic views were soundly rejected by a strong majority of Russian voters. Citing the threat from the West and the need to defend against it seemed to have reached the end of its useful life in Soviet and Russian domestic politics.

---

[16]Yevgeniy Ambartsumov, "Ne Nervnichat'!" *Literaturnaya Gazeta*, December 27, 1989.

[17]Interviews with Aleksandr Prokhanov, Viktor Alksnis, and Shamil' Sultanov, Moscow, September–October 1990 and February–March 1991.

That impression was especially reinforced after the failure of the re-actionary coup in August 1991. Boris Yeltsin and the democratic coalition came to power promising a program of sweeping changes in Russia in the area of domestic policy and publicly stated their firm commitment to a foreign and security policy seeking a rapproche-ment with the West, in general, and establishing close relations with the United States.    Particularly telling in this respect was Boris Yeltsin's choice of Yegor Gaydar to head the new government.    An economist whom the media had described as an ardent proponent of the Chicago-school monetarist brand of economics, Gaydar made no secret of his ambitious plan for reforming Russia's economy, one that included a wide-ranging program of cuts in defense spending, privatization, and integration of Russia into the world economy. Consistent with this economic ideology was the position taken by the Yeltsin coalition on relations with the former colonies:    abandon-ment of the empire and rebuilding of ties on the basis of mutual profitability.    Imperial obligations in the form of transfers and subsi-dies to the republics stood in direct contradiction to the tight-money policy advocated by Gaydar.    Russia could no longer afford an em-pire, external or internal.

Another member of Yeltsin's team was Foreign Minister Andrey Kozyrev, also known as an important player in the formulation of the Gorbachev-Shevardnadze foreign and security policies.    Kozyrev was once a protégé of former Soviet Foreign Minister Eduard Shevardnadze and a proponent of closer cooperation with the United States and Western Europe eventually leading to Russia's in-tegration into the West.    Top priority in Russia's foreign policy under the guidance of Gaydar and Kozyrev, it seemed, would be assigned to the task of integration with the West.    Other interests and regions ap-peared to have become subordinated to the overall strategic goal of Westernization of Russia's foreign policy.

Although Russia initially had not established its own Defense Ministry and had not appointed a Defense Minister, Yeltsin's even-tual choice for the post was General Pavel Grachev, who had played an important role in defeating the August coup.    Grachev's views on national security and defense policy matters were not known, but his apparent close ties to Yeltsin raised no concerns that the overall di-rection of Soviet and Russian defense and security policy would be reversed.    Moreover, the military's influence in setting national security policy had been severely eroded after years of perestroyka and the discreditation of hard-line military brass following the August coup. The key to setting Russia's foreign policy and national security course appeared to rest firmly in the hands of Russia's new political elite, who were predominantly proponents of and participants in the perestroyka-era Soviet foreign and security policies. The change in Russia's strategic direction appeared sealed.

# IN SEARCH OF NATIONAL IDENTITY AND NATIONAL INTEREST

The bulk of the intellectual baggage inherited by Yeltsin's Russia from Gorbachev's Soviet Union in the area of foreign and security policy amounted to the idea that Soviet policies of the cold war era were a mistake and that they had to be corrected. While that premise may have been sufficient to guide Soviet foreign and security policies in a period of transition and restructuring, it was not enough to guide the foreign and security policies of newly independent Russia. It was not sufficient for Russia simply to continue following the Shevardnadze-Gorbachev line, if only because Russia, having made the choice to shed its empire, found itself in a fundamentally different geopolitical situation than that of the former Soviet Union. Its new foreign policy required a new formulation and articulation of Russia's national interest that would guide its foreign and security policies.

The Shevardnadze-Gorbachev legacy was not enough to build a new foreign policy on also because that legacy lacked a vision of national interest that would serve as a solid foundation for the new policy. The legacy of the Gorbachev era to the Yeltsin administration was chiefly in clearing away the obstacles created during the cold war. But to proceed from that point, Russia had to answer the fundamental question of its national interest. Without it no foreign and security policy would be possible. Moreover, the general strategic orientation toward partnership with the West proved insufficient as the basis for Russian foreign policy. In its quest for partnership and alliance with the West, Russia could not ignore the political and economic reality of its position among the newly independent states.

Domestic politics in Russia and other ex-Soviet states (to say nothing of geography, history, and ethnicity) made it imperative that Russia turn its attention to the issue of post-Soviet settlement.

Thus, foremost among the new challenges facing Russia's policy-makers was the task of formulating Russian interests in the former republics—the newly independent states—and policies toward them. Only then the second task, in many respects equally important but largely determined by the first, would face Russian national security and foreign policymakers: Formulate Russia's interests and policies beyond the confines of its former empire and toward key powers in Europe, Asia, and the United States. Thus, geography, history, economics, and domestic politics imposed their own order on Russia's foreign policy priorities.

For Russia, emerging from centuries of its imperial and Soviet history and seeking to come to terms with that legacy, no issue was more important in the wake of the Soviet breakup than that of relations with the other former republics. Relations with these newly independent states were bound to have a profound effect on Russia's own domestic politics, strategic orientation, and quest for national identity, as well as relations with other more distant countries to which it was not bound by ties of common lineage.

Like most political programs, the "Little Russia" platform that had encountered such strong support during the political battles of the late-Soviet period and served Boris Yeltsin and his allies in the democratic coalition so well in 1991 provided only the most basic outlines of future relations with the republics. Moreover, the breathtaking speed of the dissolution of the Soviet Union, the accelerating economic crisis, and the political instability throughout the post-Soviet states, which greeted their publics and leaders at the onset of independence, combined to form a powerful obstacle to an orderly and deliberate pursuit of a post-divorce settlement among the newly independent states.

Thus, the specifics of post-Soviet settlements between Russia and the former republics occurred during tumultuous political and socio-economic conditions amid the waning euphoria of independence and its rising challenges, as the new states, including Russia, embarked on their quest for true sovereignty.

The breakup of the Soviet Union and the victory of the "Little Russia" platform occurred against the background of dissatisfaction with the *Soviet* state and its economy, as well as the background of expectations of economic improvements and greater political stability. But the details of the post-Soviet settlement and elaboration of new arrangements linking the former republics had to be accomplished in the new *Russia*, amid shattered expectations, economic hardships, and the ever-present specter of mass socioeconomic dislocation as a result of newly launched reforms.

The first few months of Russia's post-Soviet experience demonstrated how short-lived and fragile was the "Little Russia" consensus that had prevailed in Russian politics at the end of 1991 and culminated in the Commonwealth Treaty signed by the leaders of Belarus, Russia, and Ukraine. The centripetal political forces and opponents of the dissolution of the Soviet Union, which seemed defeated in the wake of the August coup, proved remarkably resilient and missed no opportunity to seek political rehabilitation, legitimacy, and a voice in the public debate about Russia's post-Soviet course.

The original and most lasting opposition to the dissolution of the Soviet Union came from an influential coalition of industrial (including defense-industrial) managers that emerged in the final year of the Gorbachev administration and had played a prominent role in the final struggle for the preservation of the centralized Soviet state. Guided by a career party apparatchik Arkadiy Volskiy, the lobby reemerged in Russian politics in the early post-Soviet period, having changed its name from the "Scientific-Industrial Union" to the "Union of Industrialists and Entrepreneurs of Russia."

Preservation of post-Soviet "common economic space" and interrepublican economic links has been one of the key items on the Union's agenda from its very beginning. The breakup of the USSR and the demise of the central planning and allocative government bodies dealt a severe blow to the already weakened industrial enterprises of Russia, many of them dependent on far-flung monopolistic producers and other vital suppliers of intermediate goods and raw materials. Thus, preservation of "common economic space," and along with it the existing *structure* of the economy, became a matter of political and economic survival for Russia's key interest group.

Driven by the desire to preserve the "common economic space" and its influence throughout the post-Soviet economy, the defense-industrialist lobby has sought an ideological rationale for its political and economic interests. Some of these efforts have bordered on the absurd. For example, Arkadiy Volskiy penned an article in *Pravda*, arguing on the basis of a study by Russian geneticists that one of the legacies of the Soviet era was the development of a new, genetically distinct type of "Soviet man," which, presumably, would justify the concept of a Soviet nation, which in turn would require the restoration of the Soviet Union as a nation-state.[1]

But in addition to Soviet-era industrial *nomenklatura* and their political leaders like Volskiy, as well as Communists and other members of the "red-brown" coalition opposed to Yeltsin and committed to the idea of restoration of the Soviet empire, the ranks of the critics of the Kozyrev foreign policy line were quickly joined by key members of Yeltsin's own political coalition who had played a pivotal role in the events leading up to the dissolution of the Soviet Union. Whether expecting a backlash against the painful policies of the new government or fearing a wave of popular nostalgia for the stability of the Soviet era in the face of post-Soviet challenges to the sovereignty and independence of the new states, or for some other reason, the newfound critics of Kozyrev's policy, who alleged neglect toward the former republics, have included such prominent members of the Yeltsin coalition as Sergey Stankevich, Yevgeniy Ambartsumov, and Vladimir Lukin.

President Yeltsin's foreign policy team was subjected to criticism not so much for the breakup of the Soviet Union as for trying to leapfrog relations with immediate neighbors and neglecting Russian interests in the newly independent states.[2] The logic of this criticism implied that Russia's real (as opposed to short-sighted, crass, financial) interests did not lie in close alliance with the West. Russia, it was argued,

---

[1]Cited in *Post-Soviet/East Europe Report*, Vol. IX, No. 35, October 6, 1992.

[2]See N. Dorofeyev, "Russia Did Not Emerge Yesterday and Will Not End Tomorrow," *Trud*, June 12, 1992; Sergey Stankevich, "No One Has Yet Been Able to Completely Exclude Force from Political Arsenal," *Izvestiya*, July 7, 1992; "Industrialists Don't Need IMF Credit," *Moskovskiy Komsomolets*, August 14, 1992; and V. T., "A. Belyakov as a New Vice Premier?" *Nezavisimaya Gazeta*, July 14, 1992. Also see commentary by A. Vasil'yev, *Komsomol'skaya Pravda*, September 3, 1992.

was a great power in its own right and would pursue its own foreign policy course, rather than merely become an ally of the United States and the West in general.

Furthermore, in the view of these critics, the Russian Foreign Ministry's preoccupation with and subservience to the West generally and the United States specifically were detrimental to Russia's interests in the "near abroad" since they prevented the institution and its leadership from formulating a policy toward the former Soviet republics that would reliably protect, from local nationalists, both Russia's interests and ethnic Russians now living abroad.

Throughout 1992 and much of 1993, the most influential critic of the Kozyrev-Yeltsin foreign policy line was a former academic and one-time Chairman of the Foreign Affairs Committee of the Russian Federation Supreme Soviet, Yevgeniy Ambartsumov. A former associate of Aleksandr Yakovlev, the principal architect of Gorbachev's reforms, a one-time prominent member of Yeltsin's political coalition, and formerly an outspoken proponent of the policy of rapprochement with the West, Ambartsumov became a key advocate of policies toward the "near and far abroad" that have been described as "enlightened imperialism."

Ambartsumov turned his position of chairman of the parliamentary foreign relations committee into a bully pulpit to attack the Foreign Ministry, which was under the leadership of Andrey Kozyrev, for alleged disregard of Russia's national interest and to articulate a radically different (from the original Yeltsin vision of "Little Russia") foreign policy and interpretation of national interest. Ambartsumov's Russia is an assertive state with great-power ambitions and traditions, a sphere of influence that covers the entire territory of the former Soviet Union, and a power that ought to be willing to violate sovereignty and challenge independence of states within its sphere of influence if they step out of bounds set by Russia. However, as an experienced ex-Soviet academic skilled in matters of propaganda and walking the fine line between the politically correct and the outrageous, Ambartsumov has always presented his vision of Russian interests and policy prescriptions so as to create an image of full compliance with international legal and moral norms and historical traditions. The rationale for his policy prescriptions toward the former Soviet republics is the sensitive issue of ethnic Russians left abroad, which includes protecting their rights against hostile nationalist local regimes and protecting Russia's interests in those regions. In a statement to the popular Moscow paper *Megapolis-Express* given in the spring of 1992, Ambartsumov said:

> In my view, Russia is undisputably something greater than the Russian Federation in its current borders. Therefore, its geopolitical interests must be seen much more broadly than they have been delineated on today's maps.
>
> Based on that we intend to build the concept of our relations with the "near abroad." Its cornerstone is the defense of national-state interests. This is not interference in the internal affairs, but defense of human rights. Our parliament will not tolerate violation of rights of ethnic Russians in the Baltic countries.
>
> We are also concerned about the situation along Russia's Southern borders. The border has moved north and geopolitical vacuum has developed in Transcaucasia. There is a danger of historical revanche. Everybody knows centuries-old conflicts between Russia and Turkey. I do not want to say that the Turkish government today wants to reclaim the Northern part of the Black Sea coast and the Crimean peninsula. But looking ahead one must keep that in mind. Vacuum is always filled by opposing forces.
>
> Our [Foreign Affairs] Committee has been critical of the government's policy in the "near abroad." I think that one must take into account much more the state-national interests of Russia.[3]

This view has been shared by others among Russia's political elite, many of them former prominent members of the democratic coalition or the progressive academic establishment. Thus, Sergey Stankevich, once a leading member of the reform faction in the USSR Supreme Soviet—the Inter-regional Group of Deputies—has called for a new foreign policy for Russia, one that would match its great-power ambitions and interests.[4] Russia's foreign policy, according to Stankevich, has been excessively influenced by the baggage left from the days of Shevardnadze; it has contained too many "smiles." That

---

[3]Yevgeniy Ambartsumov, "Interesy Rossii Ne Znayut Granits," *Megapolis-Express*, May 6, 1992.

[4]*Rossiyskaya Gazeta*, July 28, 1992, cited in RFE/RL Daily Report No. 144, July 30, 1992.

has to end. It is time to show some teeth and stand up for Russia's thousand-year-old interests and tradition of defending them.[5]

In the opinion of prominent political scientist Andranik Migranyan, formerly a political advisor to Ambartsumov and currently a member of Yeltsin's Presidential Council, Kozyrev's foreign policy is guided by a false understanding of Russia's interests. According to Migranyan, the time has come for Russia to assert itself and "let the world know where her vital interests are."[6] These vital interests are first and foremost on the territory of the former Soviet Union. Russia, in Migranyan's view,

> de jure and de facto has to play a special role throughout the Commonwealth of Independent States and the territory of the former Soviet Union.
>
> Russia must declare to the world community that the entire geopolitical space of the former USSR is the sphere of its vital interests. It does not presume the threat to use force throughout that space, it is against any conflicts and is ready to play here the role of mediator and guarantor of stability.
>
> I anticipate charges of [great-power arrogance] with respect to the [proposed] declaration of the entire former USSR [as] Russia's sphere of vital interests. [But] the United States early in the last century declared the Monroe Doctrine and asserted its special rights in the entire Western Hemisphere. Today the whole world is seen by the United States as a zone of its vital interests, including some territories of the former USSR.[7]

The Shevardnadze legacy in Russian foreign policy has become the subject of revisionist attacks. Soviet foreign policy of that era has been reconsidered by Ambartsumov, Migranyan, and quite a few of

---

[5]Sergey Stankevich, "Fenomen Derzhavy," *Rossiyskaya Gazeta*, June 23, 1992.

[6]Andranik Migranyan, "Podlinnyye I Mnimyye Orientiry Vo Vneshney Politike," *Rossiyskaya Gazeta*, August 4, 1992. This view was expanded and elaborated in considerable detail in a series of articles by Migranyan published in *Nezavisimaya Gazeta* in 1994. See Andranik Migranyan, "Rossiya i Blizhnee Zarubezh'ye: Vsyo Prostranstvo Byvshego SSSR Yavlyaetsya Sferoy Zhiznennykh Interesov Rossii," *Nezavisimaya Gazeta*, January 12 and 18, 1994.

[7]Ibid.

their colleagues in the foreign policy community as "disorderly re-
treat and complete capitulation before the West."[8]  Russia, in their
view, has retreated from its empire too soon without due attention to
its geopolitical interest.  The key goal of Russian foreign policy after
the Soviet collapse is, therefore, to reestablish its sphere of influence
and seek appropriate recognition of it and assurances of noninterfer-
ence from the G-7 countries.  Russia should become the "Eurasian
gendarme"—a function that must not only be recognized by the G-7
powers, but subsidized through hard currency grants for Russia's
contingent of rapid reaction forces necessary for protection of its interests and maintenance of law and order throughout its sphere of
influence.[9]

While the candor and terms of the vision of Russian interests and
policy prescriptions put forth by Stankevich, Ambartsumov, and
Migranyan are striking in themselves, particularly when contrasted
with the prevailing foreign policy consensus in the Russia of the
recent past, the essence of these statements is shared by a broad
segment of Russian analysts.  For example, Galina Starovoytova (who
until early 1993 held the post of Yeltsin's advisor on nationalities
problems, who has long had a reputation as a thoughtful analyst
regarding ethnic issues, and who has impeccable democratic
credentials) has articulated a similar, albeit more carefully phrased,
vision of Russian interests in the "near abroad," emphasizing the
importance of human rights to Russia.  Her proposal focused on the
idea of creating the so-called "club of civilized countries," which
would "take upon themselves the moral right to assert the new order
in the world."[10]  In other words, these "civilized nations" should
assert their right to set the rules of behavior for the rest of the world.
The right of nations to self-determination is of particular concern for
Starovoytova, who apparently believes that it is up to the civilized
nations to decide who should have that right and who should not.[11]

---

[8]Quoted in Konstantin Eggert, "Russia in the Role of 'Eurasian Gendarme?' Chairman
of Parliamentary Committee Elaborates His Foreign Policy Concept," *Izvestiya*, August
8, 1992, translated in FBIS-SOV-92-157, August 13, 1992.

[9]Ibid.

[10]"Deklaratsiya Prav Cheloveka Dolzhna Poluchit' Garantii Ot Vsekh Stran," *Izvestiya*,
August 8, 1992.

[11]Ibid.

It requires only a short analytical leap to come to the conclusion that unequivocal elevation of defense of human rights above the principle of state sovereignty would provide Russia with a legitimate cause for intervention in the "near abroad" whenever and wherever the rights of ethnic Russians are perceived to be in jeopardy. As a member of the club of civilized nations, Russia would, in effect, become the human rights "gendarme" for the former Soviet Union. Because of Russia's geographical position and the presence of ethnic Russians throughout the former USSR, the proposal would come dangerously close to legitimizing Russia's special interest and role in what the new "enlightened imperialists" would like to become Russia's sphere of vital interest and influence.

The writings of Russian academics and parliamentary figures eventually found their way into presidential rhetoric, elevating Russia's new assertiveness in the former Soviet arena to the level of an officially adopted policy line. Speaking at a congress of the Civic Union at the end of February 1993, President Boris Yeltsin declared his government's intention to seek the international community's endorsement of Russia's special rights and responsibility throughout the former Soviet Union, where it would, presumably, become the sole peacekeeper and arbiter in settling local and regional conflicts.[12] Dubbed by commentators the "Yeltsin doctrine," the speech left few doubts that Russia considered the "near abroad" its exclusive sphere of vital interests.

That conclusion was supported not only by Yeltsin's appeal to the United Nations to "grant Russia special powers as guarantor of peace and stability" in the former Soviet region, but by a subsequently elaborated Russian approach to peacekeeping operations in the CIS and Moscow's interpretation of what such operations should entail, how they ought to be initiated, and by whom they should be conducted. Russia's proposals in this area, if implemented, would establish Russia not so much as a peacekeeping element and an arm of the international community in general and the United Nations in particular, but as a gendarme with predelegated powers and authority to police the former Soviet republics. Russian official thinking in

---

[12]Serge Schmemann, "Yeltsin Suggests a Role for Russia to Keep Peace in Ex-Soviet Lands," *The New York Times*, March 1, 1993.

this area leaves little, if any, room for international intervention and peacekeeping presence in the former Soviet Union, leaving Russia, in effect, the sole enforcer and arbiter of security and stability in the region.[13]

Moreover, this Russian approach to peacekeeping is based on the assumption that Russia should be conducting such operations throughout the former Soviet Union not because it is an impartial and uninterested actor with no stake in the outcome of each individual conflict, but precisely because Russia has interests in each such conflict and nobody has greater interests in them. Hence, Russian participation presumes Moscow's role as the ultimate authority in such conflicts.

Russian thinking about peacekeeping in the former Soviet Union and attempts to codify Moscow's role as the overseer of security affairs in its "exclusive sphere of influence" with predelegated authority for intervention reflect a clearly perceptible desire for an internationally sanctioned *droit de regard* over its former colonies. As in the case of defending ethnic Russians and protecting human rights in the "near abroad," Moscow's interpretation of its peacekeeping role is only a short analytical step away from arguments about "exclusive spheres of influence" and a Russian "Monroe doctrine."

Russian rhetoric in the area of foreign and security policy has shifted noticeably, reflecting renewed interest in the old empire and a changing sense of priorities that put the "near abroad" at the top of the foreign and security policy agenda, even at the expense of relations with the "far abroad."[14]

---

[13]Suzanne Crow, "Russia Seeks Leadership in Regional Peacekeeping," *RFE/RL Research Report*, Vol. 2, No. 15, April 9, 1993.

[14]Interviews, Moscow, April–May, 1992. See also Sergey Stankevich, "Derzhava v Poiskakh Sebya," *Nezavisimaya Gazeta*, March 28, 1992; "Yavleniye Derzhavy," *Rossiyskaya Gazeta*, June 26, 1992; and Vladimir Lukin, "Rossiya i Eye Interesy," *Nezavisimaya Gazeta*, Ocotber 20, 1992.

For examples of a broad range of alternatives to the Western-oriented Russian foreign policy of the early post-Soviet period, see E. A. Pozdnyakov, "Sovremennyye Geopoliticheskiye Izmeneniya i Ikh Vliyaniye na Bezopasnost' i Stabil'nost' v Mire," *Voyennaya Mysl'*, January 1993; "Sovremennyye Geopoliticheskiye Izmeneniya i Ikh Vliyaniye na Bezopasnost' i Stabil'nost' v Mire," *Voyennaya Mysl'*, January 1993; N. Narochnitskaya, "Natsional'nyy Interes Rossii," *Mezhdunarodnaya Zhizn'*, Nos. 3–4, 1992; Boris Tarasov, "Voyennaya Strategiya Rossii: Evraziyskiy Aspekt," *Nash*

The reintegrationist theme in Russian deliberations about relations with the "near abroad" has become more pronounced during the electoral campaign for and especially since the parliamentary election of December 12, 1993. The electoral victory of the so-called "centrist" and left-wing political movements favoring preservation of a large government sector in the economy and restoration of old union links was followed by a government reshuffle that led to yet more departures—of vice premier Yegor Gaydar and finance minister Boris Fedorov—and consolidation of the industrialist lobby's hold on the upper echelons of the executive branch.

However, the arrival of the industrialist lobby at the top of Russian government and politics will not necessarily lead to an immediate and unequivocal reexpansionist Russian policy in the CIS. Russian deliberations about the country's role in the post-Soviet "geopolitical space" have reflected a great deal of ambivalence among the country's political and intellectual elite about the feasibility and advisability of the reexpansionist course for Moscow. The price of reexpansion has been deemed high—a fact that has evidently registered in the minds of some Russian policymakers.[15] Growing concerns about the costs of a new empire or sphere of influence and the price that Russia would have to pay for the privilege of recognition of its special role in "post-Soviet geopolitical space" have only underscored the dichotomy between Russian ambition with regard to the CIS and the means available to fulfill that ambition.[16]

---

*Sovremennik*, No. 12, 1992; Shamil' Sultanov, "Dukh Evraziytsa," *Nash Sovremennik*, No. 7, 1992; Kseniya Myalo, "Yest' li v Yevrazii Mesto dlya Russkikh?" *Literaturnaya Rossiya*, August 7, 1992; and N. Kosolapov, "Vneshnyaya Politika Rossii: Problemy Stanovleniya I Politikoformiruyushchiye Faktory," *Mirovaya Ekonomika i Mezhdunarodnyye Otnosheniya*, No. 2, 1993.

[15]As Russian coal miners protested government policies in Moscow, one Russian policymaker remarked in early April of 1993: "All we need now is to get saddled with [the unprofitable Ukrainian—E.R.] Donbass [coal-mining region]. As if we don't have enough problems of our own."

[16]See commentary by Pavel Fel'gengauer, "Bazy na Vynos," *Segodnya*, April 8, 1994:

"Agreements on Russian military bases (if everything that has been planned can be agreed upon) may require from Russia such expenditures that will cause greater damage to the security of the country than the loss of military bases themselves. It is entirely possible that it will be necessary to give up the comprehensive system of military bases just as Russia had to give up with regret the Combined Armed Forces of the CIS."

The costs associated with this ambition can be measured in both monetary and human terms. In human terms, Russian attempts to maintain a degree of stability in Tajikistan and to control the Tajik-Afghan border have cost the lives of dozens of Russian soldiers. The prospect of another "Afghan" is clearly not cherished either by many in the military establishment or by the population at large. The requirement to sustain peacekeeping and peacemaking operations in other parts of the CIS, including Russia's own North Caucasus, poses a serious enough challenge to the military institution and national troops, who are already reeling from budget cuts and suffering from poor morale.

In monetary terms, Russian reluctance to pay the price of its own sphere of influence has been demonstrated amply in the collapse of the ruble zone in the fall of 1993, as well as by Russian reserve at the prospect of an economic union with Belarus.[17] In both instances the threat of new pressures on Russia's treasury was evidently deemed not worth the benefit to its sphere of influence.

While some former republics and provinces of the old empire contemplate the prospect of closer cooperation with Russia, many Russians are asking themselves more and more often: Do we need this? Recent Russian debates have begun to reflect the same attitude toward such countries as Ukraine and Belarus, whose economic position, in the view of Russian analysts, is hopeless. "Who needs you?" one prominent Russian analyst told a gathering of his Ukrainian colleagues discussing Russian-Ukrainian relations. This attitude has become more and more visible among Russian analysts, who, despite the rhetoric of neoimperialism, seem to display growing concerns about the costs of reexpansion.[18]

---

[17]On this, see Andrey Grigor'yev, "Moskva Menyaet Pravila igry v Rublevoy Zone," *Segodnya*, October 30, 1993; Vitaliy Portnikov, "Kazakhstan Pokidaet Rublevuyu Zonu," *Nezavisimaya Gazeta*, November 11, 1993; Sergey Kozlov, "Moskva Postavila Alma-Ate Nepriyemlemyye Finansovyye Usloviya," *Nezavisimaya Gazeta*, November 11, 1993; and Valentin Zhdanko and Dmitriy Volkov, "Belorussia Rasschityvayet Voyti v Rublevuyu Zonu 17 Fevralya, Chego by Eto ni Stoilo Rossii," *Segodnya*, February 9, 1994.

[18]See, for example, Sergey Karaganov, "Ukraina kak Yabloko Razdora," *Moskovskiye Novosti*, April 3–10, 1994.

The prospect of a closer economic and political association between Russia on the one hand and Ukraine and Belarus on the other hand in the wake of the latter two's presidential elections has resulted in little enthusiasm, even among Moscow's most vigorous advocates of expanded Russian presence in the "near abroad." Commenting on the election of the two candidates in Kiev and Minsk who had advocated in their campaigns closer ties to Russia, Andranik Migranyan said:

> "This orientation of Ukraine and Belarus toward Russia demands certain economic concessions to these states. Taking into account the difficult situation in Russia, it is an additional strain for the Russian economy."[19]

Indeed, as the reintegrationist chorus grows louder in Russia and some other states of the former Soviet Union,[20] the economic costs of reintegration are playing an ever-growing role in deliberations about policies toward the "near abroad." Thus, the monetary union with Belarus, whose economy is falling apart and threatens Russia with an even greater burden of subsidies to inefficient industries, stumbled precisely because Russia's government is unwilling to add pressures to its already strained budget.

Thus, reality intervened at a time when Russian debates about relations with the former republics began to reach a certain consensus. This consensus reflects a great deal of interest on behalf of Russian foreign and security policy analysts and practitioners in reintegration of the "post-Soviet space" around Russia and in Russia's assuming a special role of guarantor of stability and security throughout that

---

[19]Thomas de Waal, "Fresh Challenge for Russia: Closer Slavic Ties," *The Moscow Times,* July 14, 1994.

[20]In addition to Ukraine and Belarus after their presidential elections, these include Kazakhstan, whose president, Nursultan A. Nazarbayev, put forth a major initiative for a new "Eurasian Union" in March of 1994. The proposal, which would bring together only those states that would be willing to join voluntarily in a new closer (than CIS) alliance with Russia, was rejected by president Boris Yeltsin, who has publicly expressed his contentment with the currently existing CIS, though without rejecting the idea of such a union in the future. See Arkadiy Dubnov, "Evraziyskiy Soyuz: Pochemu Seychas?" *Novoye Vremya,* No. 14, 1994; Nursultan Nazarbayev, "Soyz bez Serpa I Molota," *Moskovskiye Novosti,* No. 16, April 17–24, 1994; Sanobar Shermatova, "SNG ili SSSR?" *Moskovskiye Novosti,* No. 16, April 17–24, 1994; and Andrey Zagorskiy, "Sodruzhestvo na Rasput'ye," *Moskovskiye Novosti,* No. 16, April 17–24, 1994.

"space."   However, the outlines of that consensus have emerged amid vivid reminders of the prohibitive costs of such reexpansion and the costs' adverse effect on Russia's own economy and domestic politics.

# THE COUNCIL FOR FOREIGN AND DEFENSE POLICY: SEARCHING FOR THE MIDDLE GROUND

While much of the new foreign and security policy debate in Moscow has been colored by neoimperialist and, occasionally, anti-Western rhetoric, there has emerged a more sophisticated voice pursuing a new moderate agenda toward the West and the "near abroad." That voice belongs to a private group known as the Council for Foreign and Defense Policy. Its report, published on the first anniversary of the August coup, presented the most comprehensive and, arguably, the most balanced and sophisticated vision of Russia's national interests, emerging challenges, and solutions.[1] The report stands in stark contrast to the neoimperialist and anti-Western statements of Stankevich, Ambartsumov, and other prominent Russian politicians and academics. Nonetheless, it contains a number of policy prescriptions that could once again put Russia on a collision course with the West in dealing with both "near and far abroad." The extent to which the report represents the current consensus and to which its prescriptions are likely to be implemented in Russia's foreign and security policies remains an open question.

---

[1]"Strategiya dlya Rossii," *Nezavisimaya Gazeta*, August 19, 1992.

The council, a private group, included many prominent political personalities, senior government officials, and academics, representing various political points of view. At the time of its founding, its members included Andrey Kokoshin, first deputy minister of defense; Sergey Karaganov, deputy director of the Institute of Europe and council director; Yevgeniy Ambartsumov, then-chairman of the parliamentary foreign affairs committee; Andrey Kozyrev, the foreign minister; Sergey Yegorov, president of the Association of Russian Banks; and Mark Masarskiy, president of the Association of Leaders of Enterprises.

Many of the report's authors had played an active role in the Gorbachev-era foreign and security policy debates.

The report's authors take for granted that close cooperation and partnership with the West is in Russia's best interest in the long term. But they also note that the chances of such an alliance in the near future are slim, given the numerous internal and external political, security, and economic challenges to Russia and its limited ability to cope with them. The report argues that Russia has to scale back its great-power "geostrategic" ambitions, especially when it comes to overseas commitments, and return to what its authors describe as Russia's traditional continental strategy. The return to that strategy is dictated by the numerous new challenges to Russia's national security from the territory of the former Soviet Union.

The strategy toward the former Soviet republics, chosen by the report's authors—"Post-Imperial Enlightened Integration"—represents a balanced treatment of Russia's legitimate interests in—and relations with—the former republics. But even it carries implicitly the idea of a Russian de facto sphere of interests throughout the former Soviet Union, as well as the specter of Russian reexpansion. The authors of the report describe as "essential" the task of building a new strategic partnership with the West in which Russia would play an important role, "regulating the situation in Eastern Europe, Central Asia and the Far East."

The "enlightened post-imperial course" advocated in the report should build new interstate structures and build a new commonwealth actively participating (and, to the extent possible, internationally sanctioned) in conflict prevention, if necessary with the help of military forces, and preventing large-scale human rights' violations. The authors advocate that Russia not exclude, under extraordinary circumstances, the possibility of unilateral actions—political and economic sanctions and, in extreme cases, even direct intervention by force.

The authors of "Strategiya dlya Rossii" emphasize, however, that defense of human rights should be of paramount importance not only with respect to ethnic Russians abroad, but to all other groups suffering persecution. Although the report hints at a special role for Russia in post-Soviet Central Eurasia, it suggests that the rationale for this role can be found not in visions of Russia's inherent superiority or presumed historical rights, but rather in the OSCE (Organization on

Security and Cooperation in Europe) charter and in international law.

While implicitly asserting Russia's special role on the territory of the former Soviet Union, the report emphasizes economic and political integration and cooperation with the former republics, rather than overt political and military pressure to bring them back into Russia's orbit. The key elements of such a course should, in the view of the report's authors, be based on the following principles:

- Unconditional recognition of the inviolability of the existing borders, despite their obviously artificial nature.

- Emphasis on building a network of constantly functioning interstate bodies regulating relations in economics, transport, energy, finance, education, culture, and defense.

- Triple alliance with key states: Belarus, Kazakhstan, and—in the Caucasus—Georgia.

- Encouragement of Russian state and private investment in the countries of the "near abroad." Investment expansion will not only serve as a source of commercial revenues but will provide additional political influence and strengthen forces interested in establishing an effective commonwealth.

Turning their attention beyond the "near abroad," the authors of the report emphasize the need for diversity and balance in Russia's foreign policy. That balance is reflected in their sober and realistic assessment of Russia's interests vis-à-vis the United States, Europe, and Asia, an assessment devoid of the paranoia and xenophobia that have permeated many recent Russian statements on relations with countries outside the "near abroad."[2] The thrust of the arguments contained in the report is that good relations with the West should not be seen as a panacea for Russia's domestic troubles, nor should they come at the expense of or infringe upon Russia's relations with other powers in Europe or Asia.

---

[2]See for example, N. Narochnitskaya, "Natsional'nyy Interes Rossii," *Mezhdunarodnaya Zhizn'*, No. 3–4, 1992.

The lack of military threat from the West is duly and prominently acknowledged by the report's authors. However, the report reflects concerns about instability and geopolitical vacuum around Russia's periphery. Cooperation with the sole remaining superpower—the United States—in meeting the challenge of instability is recognized in the report. However, partnership with the United States is not regarded as the sole solution to Russia's security challenges.

The report reflects a distinct Eurocentric bias among its authors and recognition of Europe's importance for Russia's long-term interests. However, its authors are fully aware of the obstacles facing Russia on the road to rapprochement with Europe and recognize the need to search for alternative partners in economic development in Asia.

Notwithstanding these obstacles, the report clearly reflects its authors' conviction that a European orientation must remain the key strategic direction of Russia's foreign and security policy. And no states are more important, in their view, to European security, stability, and Russia's interests on the continent than Germany and the United States. Cooperation and partnership with them, according to the authors, must remain key elements of Russia's foreign and security policy.

Impressive in terms of its overall breadth and balance, the council's report devotes considerable attention to Russian defense policy. The following issues are seen by its authors as key to Russia's internal and external security:

- Restoration of political control over the military institution and preservation of its integrity
- Transition from a conscript-based force to contract service
- Reduction in the overall size of the military establishment
- Preservation of core defense-industrial and research and development potential at the expense of current procurement
- Establishment of rapid-reaction forces for domestic contingencies and crises around Russia's perimeter
- Preservation of strategic nuclear capabilities necessary for, but not exceeding the requirements of, strategic stability; elimination of tactical nuclear weapons.

The report also calls for the establishment of an "integrated early warning, control and unauthorized launch prevention system," as well as regional ballistic missile defense systems. At the same time, fundamental revisions of the Antiballistic Missile Treaty and creation of global ballistic missile defenses are not recommended.

The report of the Council for Foreign and Defense Policy deserves special attention because it represents the most comprehensive and responsible assessment of Russia's challenges in the area of foreign policy and national security. It also articulates a vision that is free from early post-Soviet euphoria and offers a balanced strategy for dealing with these challenges.

In May 1994, the council issued a follow-up report, reaffirming its position as perhaps the most influential public Russian organization devoted to issues of national security and foreign policy and, once again, demonstrating its aspiration to the centrist and balanced position on many controversial issues on Russia's crowded foreign and security policy agenda.[3] Noting shifts in Russian public opinion and the vector of debates on foreign and security policy, the second report's authors express that, while their first statement published in 1992 was intended to bring balance to Russian foreign and security policy and awaken policymakers to the need to devote greater attention to matters of post-Soviet settlement and relations with former Soviet republics, their latest contribution is meant to flag their growing concern that

> the pendulum of Russian public opinion is already swinging past the "golden middle" and moving toward a policy that is potentially far more dangerous than the one that was conducted in 1991–1992.[4]

Citing their dissatisfaction with "growing xenophobia" and the "great-power rhetoric" aimed by senior government officials primarily at a domestic audience, the report's authors maintain that such rhetoric and ambition can only heighten suspicions about Russia's imperial revanchism in both the near and far abroad. Meanwhile, the report's authors argue, Russia has broken its long-standing pat-

---

[3]See "Strategiya dlya Rossii (2)," *Nezavisimaya Gazeta*, May 27, 1994.
[4]Ibid.

tern of confrontation with and isolation from the outside world and for the foreseeable future has no enemies, which is a "gigantic advantage" in its geostrategic position.[5]

On the crucial question of relations with the "near abroad," the report's authors have emphasized that Russia currently does not have the resources—economic, political, or military—to play the role of guarantor of the stability of its neighbors, which are struggling with the challenge of post-Soviet transition.    But it would also be unrealistic for Russia to try to escape the predicament that has been determined by its historical, political, and geographic ties to the former republics.[6]

Hence, Russia, in the view of the report's authors, has little latitude when it comes to choosing its strategic course in relation to the "near abroad." Even limited attempts at reintegration of the former Soviet republics around Russia could, in their view, have negative consequences for Russia's economy and domestic politics. Russia must be extremely selective in responding to integrationists pressures from within and outside. In pursuing this course Russia

> must be only for such integration that will be profitable for it. The right to a policy of "enlightened selfishness" should also be recognized for our neighbors. . . .  The philosophy of this approach [should be] "leadership instead of direct control."[7]

Although Russia's political future and its strategic orientation remain uncertain, two matters have become clear since the breakup of the Soviet Union.  First, the unequivocally pro-Western orientation of Russian foreign policy that marked the early post-Soviet period is a thing of the past.  Second, Russia cannot escape its geography and history.  Its foreign policy will have to deal with the "near abroad" in a more active manner than was implicit in the policy of "benign neglect" of the early years of the Yeltsin period.  More often than not, policy toward the "near abroad" will be made under the influence of

---

[5]Ibid.
[6]Ibid.
[7]Ibid.

domestic political and economic interests and often will be tinged with overtones of neoimperialism and great-power chauvinism.

Given the correlation of forces in Russian domestic politics after the December 1993 election and the government reshuffle in January 1994, one can predict with a high degree of confidence that Russian interests in the "near abroad" will dominate the country's foreign policy agenda. As evidenced by Georgia's and Azerbaijan's joining the CIS; Russia's negotiation of a special treaty providing for economic integration between Russia and Belarus; Russia's protection of Russians in the "near abroad," as pledged by President Yeltsin in his televised New Year's Eve address on December 31, 1993; and Russia's continuing military presence in the "near abroad" for fear that the vacuum will be filled by hostile forces, as envisioned by Foreign Minister Andrey Kozyrev; restoration of intra-Commonwealth links promises to figure prominently on Russia's foreign policy agenda. The essence of the Civic Union's program and recommendations put forth by the Council for Foreign and Defense Policy are now becoming Russian policy. If the policy is executed with the degree of skill, moderation, and political tact reflected in the council's report, the worst excesses of Russian neoimperialist rhetoric will likely remain just that.

Amid this wide-ranging debate on Russian national interest and national security policy, the two institutions that were formally entrusted with the formulation and conduct of that policy have remained passive. The Ministry of Foreign Affairs and the Ministry of Defense did little to contribute to the debate and, at times, have been completely overshadowed by academics and parliamentarians who were eager to express yet another point of view on Russia's national security requirements. The two critical institutions have stayed largely out of the public debate on national interest and national security, confining their views on the subject to bland official documents, such as the "Concept of Russian Foreign Policy,"[1] or "Russian Military Doctrine."[2]

If the Ministry of Foreign Affairs' institutional position on national interest and national security was ever presented to a general audience, it came in the form of occasional statements in the media and interviews by Foreign Minister Andrey Kozyrev.[3]

---

[1]"Kontseptsiya Vneshney Politiki Rossiyskoy Federatsii," January 25, 1993. Translated in FBIS-USR-93-037, March 25, 1993.

[2]*Rossiyskiye Vesti*, November 18, 1993.

[3]Other senior representatives of the Ministry of Foreign Affairs have on occasion taken part in articulation of Russia's foreign policy, in particular in defense of the ministry's policy toward the "near abroad," but this was not done consistently and was largely a reaction to charges of incompetence or even treason leveled against the ministry by its detractors. For example, see the remarks of Fyodor Shelov-Kovedyaev, Kozyrev's one-time first deputy responsible for Russian policy toward the "near abroad," in *Nezavisimaya Gazeta*, July 30, 1992. For an expanded version of these remarks, see

The record of Kozyrev's statements on foreign and security policy is mixed and appears to have shifted away from the early post-Soviet, pro-Western course whose authorship has often been ascribed to him by both his critics and supporters. One of the most forceful statements by Kozyrev in defense of Russia's quest for partnership with the West came in the summer of 1992. Kozyrev said that Russia has no choice but to pursue a close alliance with the West that will enable it to become the critical link between the East and the West, owing to its critical geographic and cultural position. To turn away from the West, in Kozyrev's view, would mean losing a precious opportunity and leaving Russia forever as the "sick man of Europe."[4] The "Western direction," according to Kozyrev, is the top priority of Russian foreign policy.[5]

But Kozyrev's sense of priorities in Russian foreign policy evidently has changed as a function of the domestic political climate. Even to an untrained observer the foreign minister's statements on key directions in Russian foreign policy would at times appear contradictory. Thus, while declaring partnership with the West as the undisputed top priority of Russian foreign policy in the summer of 1992, Kozyrev suggested that Russia should not follow the lead of the Western alliance in the Yugoslav crisis and should "play solo more often."[6]

Unmistakable signs of changes in Kozyrev's views on priorities in Russian foreign policy and relations with the West have emerged over time as the center of gravity in Russian domestic politics has shifted. Thus, the removal of Yegor Gaydar from the government in December 1992 was followed by Kozyrev's startling speech at a CSCE meeting in Stockholm filled with irredentist ambition. Subsequently retracted and described by the foreign minister himself as a reminder to the West of what a real hard-line Russian foreign policy might look like, the speech sent shivers throughout the "near abroad" and other

---

Fyodor Shelov-Kovedyaev, *Vyzov Vremeni: Politika Novoy Rossii*, Moscow, Slovo Publishers, 1993.

[4]Andrey Kozyrev, "Preobrazheniye ili Kafkianskaya Metamorfoza," *Nezavisimaya Gazeta*, August 20, 1992.

[5]Ibid.

[6]Andrey Kozyrev, "Rossii Nado Chashche Ispolnyat' Solo," *Novoye Vremya*, No. 23, 1992.

neighbors of Russia and was taken in some capitals as a sign of future Russian policies to come.[7]

The clearest correction in Kozyrev's original foreign policy course was introduced by the foreign minister himself after the December 1993 parliamentary elections. Referring to the setback of the democratic coalition in the election, Kozyrev made it clear that changes must be made in Russian foreign policy in response to the voters' political preferences. According to the minister, these would entail the following measures: Top priority in Russian foreign policy would be given to the goal of defending the rights of Russians in the "near abroad"; the CIS would be declared the sphere of Russia's vital interests; and Russia should maintain military presence in regions that have been "the sphere of Russian interests for centuries."[8]

Minister Kozyrev's statement about the impending correction of the course of Russian foreign policy was met with unequivocal approval at the second institution whose task it is to be concerned with Russian national· security—the Ministry of Defense. Not a minute too soon, commented the ministry's newspaper, *Red Star*, in a front-page article published the day after Kozyrev's statement. "The near abroad was, is and will be the sphere of vital interests of Russia," read the headline in *Red Star* on January 20, 1994.

> The "i's" have been dotted, the priorities of Russian foreign policy have been named. Speaking about them, Russia's Foreign Minister noted that Russia "must preserve its military presence in regions that have been in its sphere of interests for centuries."[9]

Notwithstanding the military establishment's endorsement of the revised Russian foreign policy priorities, the Ministry of Defense, as an institution, has largely refrained from active participation in the debate about Russia's national interest and national security requirements. Although the ministry's media outlets, such as the daily *Red Star* and the once-classified military-theoretical monthly *Mili-*

---

[7]See Interfax, December 14, 1992; Suzanne Crow, "Competing Blueprints for Russian Foreign Policy," *RFE/RL Research Reports*, December 18, 1992.

[8]*Nezavisimaya Gazeta*, January 20, 1994; *The Moscow Times*, January 20, 1994.

[9]Vladimir Gavrilenko, "Blizhnee Zarubezh'ye Was, Is and Will Be the Sphere of Vital Interests of Russia," *Krasnaya Zvezda*, January 20, 1994.

*tary Thought*, have frequently published popular and academic articles on Russia's national security policy, its geopolitical interests, and threats from the "near and far abroad," few of them represent the ministry's official position. Judging by *Red Star*'s reaction to Kozyrev's statements on new directions in Russian foreign policy, the military institution shares the foreign minister's newly found concern about Russia's interests in the "near abroad" and Russian compatriots left there. But the ministry's top leader, specifically Defense Minister Pavel Grachev, has abstained from articulating comparable views in public.

The most important official document from the military institution was Russia's new military doctrine, which was adopted in early November 1993. The doctrine was published a few weeks later.[10]

Devoid of the rhetoric about Russia's strategic position, geopolitical interests, and inalienable rights in the "near abroad," the text of the doctrine demonstrates that the concerns of the Russian military establishment are focused on the immediate periphery of the country. Thus, the military establishment has followed the vector of public debates about Russia's national security interests and requirements.

The third and most outspoken institution participating in the debate about Russia's national security and national interest has been the parliament. The debate was spearheaded by the old Supreme Soviet, particularly its Foreign Affairs Committee. There is every reason to expect that the new parliament's (Duma) Foreign Affairs Committee will be just as outspoken.

The Supreme Soviet's committee was first chaired by Vladimir Lukin, a well-known academic from the elite Institute for the USA and Canada Studies. Appointed by Boris Yeltsin to serve as Russia's ambassador in Washington, Lukin was replaced by another well-known academic and one-time prominent member of the Democratic Russia movement, Yevgeniy Ambartsumov. Both were reelected to the new parliament in December 1993 on the moderate/liberal ticket headed by economist Grigoriy Yavlinskiy. Lukin has resigned from his post in Washington and once again has been elected to chair the Foreign Affairs Committee.

---

[10]"Voyennaya Doktrina Rossii," *Rossiyskiye Vesti*, November 18, 1993.

Both Lukin and Ambartsumov have been outspoken critics of the Foreign Ministry and Andrey Kozyrev. Kozyrev and the ministry led by him, they have charged, are too eager to curry favors with the West and have neglected Russia's traditional interests and allies.[11]

Russian foreign policy, charged Kozyrev's parliamentary critics, was not devoting enough attention to Russia's immediate neighbors in the "near abroad" and was too subservient to the West in general and the United States in particular. The crisis in the former Yugoslavia and Kozyrev's acceptance of the West's condemnation of Russia's traditional ally Serbia resulted in some of the most severe criticism of the foreign minister by Russian parliamentarians. Serbia, they charged, was merely one of the parties in that war, singled out unfairly by Western media as a scapegoat; Kozyrev's support for sanctions against Serbia went against traditional Russian interests in the Balkans.

Except for criticizing Kozyrev and the Ministry of Foreign Affairs for their handling of Russian foreign policy, the successive parliaments have done little to promote an alternative agenda for Russian foreign policy or a different vision of Russian national interest. This agenda and vision can be gleaned only by implication from a variety of general statements by successive Foreign Affairs Committee Chairmen Ambartsumov and Lukin. Thus, Russia should articulate for the rest of the world a "Monroe doctrine" that would declare the entire territory of the former USSR its exclusive sphere of interests and influence. Protection of rights of ethnic Russians and Russian-speakers in the "near abroad" is of paramount importance for Russia. The former Soviet republics should be made aware of that. Russia should not seek a special relationship with the West. Rather, it should balance the "Western direction" of its policy with renewed ties to China.

---

[11]Vladimir Lukin, "Rossiya i Eye Interesy," *Nezavisimaya Gazeta*, Ocotber 20, 1992; Yevgeniy Ambartsumov, "Interesy Rossii Ne Znayut Granits," *Megapolis-Express*, May 6, 1992; Konstantin Eggert, "Russia in the Role of 'Eurasian Gendarme?' Chairman of Parliamentary Committee Elaborates His Foreign Policy Concept," *Izvestiya*, August 8, 1992, translated in FBIS-SOV-92-157, August 13, 1992; "Pis'mo v Redaktsiyu Predsedatelya Komiteta VS RF po Mezhdunarodnym Delam i Vneshneekonomicheskim Svyazyam Yevgeniya Ambartsumova," *Izvestiya*, August 25, 1992; and Vladimir Lukin, "Rossiya i Eye Interesy," *Nezavisimaya Gazeta*, October 20, 1992. Also see Suzanne Crow, "Competing Blueprints for Russian Foreign Policy," *RFE/RL Research Report*, Volume 1, No. 50, December 18, 1992.

Improved relations with China will enable Russia to achieve equilibrium in its policy toward Europe and the United States.[12]

In their essence, blueprints emanating from the legislature would hardly steer Russian foreign policy along a very different course from the one it is currently pursuing. The "near abroad" has been declared the sphere of Russian special interest, and Moscow has sought special powers of intervention in that sphere from the international community. Improved relations with China have been pursued, largely through the vehicle of arms sales. Regarding the former Yugoslavia, Russia has made known its opposition to external military intervention. President Boris Yeltsin has expressed his dissatisfaction with NATO's lack of consultations prior to the air strikes in Bosnia in April 1994. And in the matter of protecting the interests of ethnic Russians in the "near abroad," Kozyrev has made it clear that few issues matter to him and his staff more than the well-being and dignity of his compatriots remaining in the former republics.

The return of Ambartsumov and Lukin to the legislature and the election of an outspoken nationalist slate to the new parliament suggest that the honeymoon in Russia's relations with the West in general and the United States in particular is over. With the legislature largely setting the rhetorical and ideological tone of the discourse and the Ministries of Foreign Affairs and of Defense pursuing a more assertive agenda in the "near abroad," the vigorously pro-Western phase of Russian foreign policy has ended.

---

[12]Vladimir Lukin, "Rossiya i Eye Interesy," *Nezavisimaya Gazeta,* October 20, 1992.

THE NATO CONSENSUS

## A CONFUSED BEGINNING

The impression that Russian foreign and security policy was moving toward a consensus was reinforced at the end of 1993 when Moscow was confronted with yet another crisis in its relations with Western and Eastern Europe, as well as the United States. The crisis was triggered by the determined drive of three of Moscow's former satellites—Poland, the Czech Republic, and Hungary—for membership in NATO.

Russia's foreign policy and security establishment was evidently unprepared to deal with the issue of NATO's eastward expansion when it moved to the top of the Russian diplomatic agenda late in the summer of 1993. During the August 1993 visit to Poland by President Boris Yeltsin, the issue of Poland's membership in NATO was raised by President Lech Walesa and met with a surprisingly favorable response from the Russian president. The official declaration issued by the two parties at the end of the summit referred to "the understanding from President B. N. Yel'tsin" of Poland's intention to join NATO, as consistent in the long term with "the interests of Russia."[1]

Yeltsin's acquiescence to Poland's desire for NATO membership was followed by a vigorous campaign conducted by the Russian diplomatic establishment aimed at overturning the Russian president's remarks in Warsaw. The then–Foreign Affairs Committee Chairman Yevgeniy Ambartsumov openly claimed that Yeltsin had been unpre-

---

[1]ITAR-TASS, August 25, 1993.

pared to deal with the issue and did not present Russia's position correctly.[2] Russia's ambassador to Poland maintained that Yeltsin's remark had been misinterpreted. Foreign Minister Kozyrev and Defense Minister Grachev issued similar statements seeking to dilute the effect of Yeltsin's remarks.[3]

Finally, Yeltsin himself went on record a month after his visit to Warsaw to reverse, in effect, his previous apparent consent to NATO's eastward expansion. A letter addressed by Yeltsin to the leaders of the United States, France, Germany, and Great Britain asserted that any eastward move by NATO can occur only after Russia itself joins the alliance and not unless Russia's security interests have been adequately assured.[4]

The prospect of NATO admission of former Warsaw Pact allies elicited an unequivocally negative reaction from Russian military and civilian security analysts across the political spectrum. Opposition to Eastern Europe's membership in NATO brought together—albeit for entirely different reasons—the few remaining outspoken proponents of Russia's close partnership with the West with critics of adopting Western policies toward Russia and the former Soviet Union, as well as neoimperialists eager to reestablish Russia's lost sphere of influence in Eastern Europe.

From the point of view of the liberal proponents of Western-oriented Russian foreign policy, Eastern and Central European states' intention to join the Western alliance would result in the establishment of yet another partition in Europe. The old "Iron Curtain" would be recreated along Poland's border with Belarus. A new formidable obstacle to Russia's integration in the Western community would thus be created, since Russia would never be admitted into NATO, according to these liberal proponents. In the opinion of one of the most vigorous proponents of closer partnership with the Western alliance, Eastern Europe's desire for Western security guarantees is entirely justifiable and understandable, but premature nonetheless:

---

[2]Cited in Suzanne Crow, "Russian Views on an Eastward Expansion of NATO," *RFE/RL Research Report*, October 15, 1993.

[3]Ibid.

[4]Ibid.

Eastern Europe should do everything to be ready to get into NATO should reforms fail here at home. It should do everything to get in the day after things go wrong here. But it should not hurry into NATO now and unless and until the reactionaries come to power here in Moscow.[5]

Others, espousing more moderate views, have also been critical of the idea of NATO's eastward expansion. It would, in their view, and depending on their analysis of the security environment in Eastern Europe, lead to one or more of the following:

- Isolation of Russia from the rest of Europe

- Establishment of a Western-allied border around Russia

- Tilting of the balance in Europe in favor of Germany.[6]

The prospect of NATO's expansion triggered a rare official public commentary from Russia's Foreign Intelligence Service—a successor to the KGB in the area of foreign intelligence headed by long-time foreign policy expert Yevgeniy Primakov.[7] The document offered an overview of key aspects of the general problem of NATO's eastward expansion and its effect on Russia's interests. Generally reserved and neutral in its assessments, the paper concluded that NATO's expansion would negatively affect Russia's military security, foreign policy, and geopolitical interests in Eastern and Central Europe, as well as meet with a negative domestic political reaction in Russia. NATO's expansion would be premature at best, concluded the document's authors.[8]

The debate about NATO was important from the point of view of Russian deliberations about national security in several respects:  It

---

[5]Interviews, Moscow, June 1993.

[6]Aleksey Pushkov, "Building a New NATO at Russia's Expense," *Foreign Affairs*, January/February 1994; Sergey Karaganov, "Rasshireniye NATO Vedet k Izolyatsii Rossii," *Moskovskiye Novosti*, September 19, 1993; Dmitriy Vol'sky, "Lugar vs. Lugar, NATO vs. NATO," *New Times*, No. 35, 1993; Vyacheslav Yelagin, "Chego Ne Ponyaly v Varshave?" *Segodnya*, September 14, 1993; and interviews, Moscow, June 1993 and November 1993.

[7]Sluzhba Vneshney Razvedki Rossiyskoy Federatsii, "Perspektivy Rasshireniya NATO i Interesy Rossii," Moscow, 1993.

[8]Ibid.

reminded Russia's foreign policy and national security community once again that Russia's security begins at its doorstep and will depend more on relations with its neighbors than on overarching designs for common European security; Russia's relations with its immediate neighbors will, to a significant extent, color links with more distant powers, especially the key powers of the Western alliance—Germany and the United States. The NATO episode demonstrated to the Russian security establishment once again that Eastern and Central Europe will continue to play a critical role in Moscow's relations with the rest of the continent, as either the bridge or the barrier between Europe's two halves.

Along with the importance of Central and Eastern Europe for Russian security interests, the controversy over "near abroad" countries joining NATO has demonstrated to Russia's national security and foreign policy community the depth of divisions in Europe and the obstacles Russia will face if it continues its westward progress. The mistrust of Russian intentions—the resilience of cold war–era fears and suspicions in Western and Central Europe and throughout the NATO community—has sent a powerful signal to Moscow that if integration into the Western community is pursued, it will be difficult, and any partnership will remain uncertain at best for a considerable period of time.

## THE PARTNERSHIP FOR PEACE—A LUKEWARM PARTNERSHIP

The NATO controversy was followed by an equally active discussion in the Russian foreign and security policy community about participation in the Partnership for Peace (PFP) plan. The issue came to the top of the Russian policy agenda after the election of the new parliament—the election in which the original radical reformist coalition led by Yegor Gaydar suffered a major setback, yielding to a far more pronounced nationalist presence in the new legislature, which was personified most vividly by Vladimir Zhirinovskiy, but which also included communists, agrarians, and even moderate reformers from the ranks of the old Democratic Russia movement.[9]  Thus, the

---

[9]These include Sergey Shakhray's Party of Russian Unity and Accord; members of Yavlinskiy's block, Vladimir Lukin and Yevgeniy Ambartsumov; and others.

Russian foreign policy establishment turned its attention to PFP after a major shift in Russian domestic politics, during a period when reform "romanticism" of any kind had already become a thing of the past.

Few Russian opponents of the plan have been able to articulate a set of concrete objections to membership in PFP. Partly this is undoubtedly due to the vague nature of the PFP agreement, which is designed to meet the individual conditions of each member-state. But several outspoken critics of PFP have raised general philosophical objections to the deal that would, in spirit, run counter to what they see as the proper course for Russian foreign and security policy. Thus, to the advocates of Russia's "Monroe doctrine," PFP

> contains an objective attempt to block the process of military-political consolidation of the space of the former Soviet Union.[10]

The program, seen by these analysts as an intermediate step to Eastern European countries' full membership in NATO, would lead to the isolation of Russia at worst, or at best, leave Russia "waiting outside" as a "junior partner" when key policy decisions are being made. Thus, by joining PFP, Russia would compromise its great-power status, weaken its own sphere of influence within the CIS, and deny itself the strategic freedom of action in pursuit of its interests.[11]

Despite their criticism of PFP, few Russian analysts spoke out unequivocally in opposition to joining the program. The single most important obstacle to Russia's rejection of the proposal lay in the argument that such a move would isolate Russia even more than Eastern European countries' membership in NATO.[12] Hence, endorsements of Russian membership in PFP have been accompanied

---

[10]Andranik Migranyan, "Zashem Vstupat', Yesli Mozhno ne Vstupat'?" *Nezavisimaya Gazeta*, March 15, 1994.

[11]Ibid.; Mikhail Karpov, "Amerika Gotova Protivostoyat' 'Russkomu 'Neoimperializmu'," *Nezavisimaya Gazeta*, April 6, 1994; Ivan Rodin, "Budushchee SNG i 'Partnerstvo vo Imya Mira'," *Nezavisimaya Gazeta*, April 15, 1994; and Vyacheslav Nikonov, "Partnerstvo vo Imya Mira," *Nezavisimaya Gazeta*, April 7, 1994.

[12]Manki Ponomarev, "Chemu Prizvano Sluzhit' 'Partnerstvo vo Imya Mira'," *Krasnaya Zvezda*, March 29, 1994; Vyacheslav Nikonov, "Partnerstvo vo Imya Mira," *Nezavisimaya Gazeta*, April 7, 1994; and Sergey Yushenkov, "'Partnerstvo vo Imya Mira'—Eto Chast' Obshchey Systemy Bezopasnosti," *Rossiyskiye Vesti*, March 26, 1994.

by amendments and caveats that, in the view of their authors, would ensure that Russian security interests and special status as a great power would be duly acknowledged by all sides.[13] Even the most outspoken early critics of PFP, such as Chairman of the Parliamentary Foreign Affairs Committee Vladimir Lukin, who had initially referred to NATO's invitation to Moscow to join PFP as "rape," have expressed lukewarm recognition of the utility of Russian participation.[14]

The lukewarm nature of Russian acceptance of PFP has been further demonstrated by Russian attempts to attach special conditions to Moscow's participation in the program, conditions designed to obtain recognition by NATO of Russia's special enhanced status.[15] Such insistence on recognition of Moscow's special status follows in the footsteps of President Boris Yeltsin's assertion of Russia's special role throughout the former Soviet Union in his Civic Union speech in February 1993, as well as appeals for a Russian "Monroe Doctrine" made by prominent Russian analysts. The quest for special status also reflects the degree to which the Russian foreign policy community has come to a consensus in its great-power ambition.

Additional signs of reluctance to endorse the program have been manifested by the uncertainty surrounding the date of Russian signing of the agreement. Initial plans to sign the agreement in April 1992 ran counter to the presidential spokesman's suggestion that Moscow might take another six or seven months to evaluate and join PFP.

The atmosphere surrounding the question of Russian participation in PFP was further clouded by Moscow's official reaction to NATO air strikes against Bosnian Serbs in April 1994. Widespread Russian objections to the air strikes, as allegedly a unilateral U.S./NATO action, focused on the lack of prior consultation with Moscow by the allies and prospective partners. The air strikes were thus seen as evidence that the West was not seriously entertaining the idea of partnership

---

[13]Ibid.

[14]"Rossiya i NATO—Ravnopravnyye Partnery," *Nezavisimaya Gazeta*, April 10, 1994.

[15]"Yel'tsin o Partnerstve v NATO," *Nezavisimaya Gazeta*, April 9, 1994; and "Boris Yel'tsin—Za Spetsial'noye Soglasheniye s NATO," *Izvestiya*, April 7, 1994.

and cooperation with Russia. Commenting on the strikes in the respected weekly *Moscow News*, Yevgeniy Ambartsumov wrote:

> Washington's actions undoubtedly compromise Russian cooperation with the West and help the national-radicals opposed to Yel'tsin. . . . What will it be like for Russian representatives to sign "Partnership for Peace" with NATO under the echo of these air strikes? Or, perhaps, the link between the events is precisely in the desire to disrupt the signing and push Russia aside?[16]

PFP was the most obvious collateral casualty in the Russian political arena of NATO air strikes. The air strikes were quickly followed by reports from the Russian Ministry of Foreign Affairs about the postponement of Andrey Kozyrev's visit to Brussels to sign the PFP agreement.[17]

Defense Minister Pavel Grachev went even further, arguing that Russia should reconsider its decision to join PFP. According to Grachev, the air strikes demonstrated that, for the West, partnership with Russia is merely an empty word. While avoiding an outright rejection of PFP, Grachev suggested that its signing may well be postponed indefinitely.[18]

The Bosnian air strikes controversy put another obstacle in the way of Russia's already reluctant and decelerating movement toward a partnership with the West. The general concept of such a partnership had already suffered from changes in Russian domestic politics that had supplanted the early post-Soviet Westernizing "romanticism" with a more assertive, nationalist vision of Russian national interest and a more "pragmatic," at best, attitude toward the West. In describing U.S. Defense Secretary William Perry's view of PFP, one Russian commentator writing in the *Red Star* referred to it as a "pragmatic partnership" designed to safeguard against the worst, yet

---

[16]Yevgeniy Ambartsumov, "Echo Bosniyskikh Bombezhek," *Moscow News*, No. 15, 1994; for a similar reaction see the comments of Sergey Shakhray, who likened the air strikes to a slap in the face of Russia, "Nam Nanesli Poshchechinu," *Trud*, April 13, 1994.

[17]"Deystviya NATO v Bosnii i Gertsgovine Pugayut Rossiyu," *Segodnya*, April 14, 1994; and Irina Grudinina, "Partnerstvo ne Otmenyayetsya—Poskol'ku ne Ob'yavlyalos'," *Segodnya*, April 15, 1994.

[18]David Filipov, "Grachev Urges NATO Rethink," *The Moscow Times*, April 16, 1994.

leaving doors open for the better. The author concluded, "Evidently, precisely this formula can become the basis for building Russian policy toward the United States."[19]

This theme was echoed in the statement of the chairman of the Duma's committee on defense, Sergey Yushenkov, who endorsed Russian participation in PFP as, in effect, the least harmful of all possible outcomes. Recognizing that Russian refusal to sign the agreement would leave his country in isolation, Yushenkov recommended signing the general framework agreement since it would imply few, if any, commitments on Russia's part. "The Russian side itself will decide later what real meaning to invest in the agreement," he said.[20]

The NATO-PFP debate has thus become another piece of the emerging mosaic of post-Soviet Russian foreign policy. By the time this controversy emerged, the process of dismantling the early Westernizing consensus was already under way. That consensus was being replaced by a more independent, perhaps even isolationist, policy that would put far greater emphasis on the task of rebuilding Russia's sphere of influence around its periphery than on integration with the more distant Western alliance. That change of emphasis in Russian foreign policy would not necessarily put Russia on a path of confrontation with the Western alliance, but it would rearrange priorities on Russia's foreign policy agenda. It would also underscore the importance of the "near abroad" for Russia in its own right, as well as create a prism through which its relations with the "far abroad," especially with the Western alliance, would be viewed.

---

[19]Mikhail Pogorelyy, "Formula 'Pragmaticheskogo Partnerstva' Rasshifrovana Yeye Zhe Avtorom," *Krasnaya Zvezda*, April 13, 1994.

[20]Dmitriy Kuznets, "Prisoyedinenye k 'Partnerstvu Nichego Ne Znachit," *Segodnya*, April 19, 1994.

# CONCLUSIONS AND POLICY IMPLICATIONS

Russian thinking on foreign and security policy is showing the signs of a fundamental shift. The consensus of the Gorbachev and Yeltsin eras that had promised to launch the Soviet Union and Russia on the path of strategic rapprochement and even partnership with the Western alliance has been replaced by a new consensus. This new consensus puts far less emphasis on the maintenance of a cooperative partnership with the West, promising to push Russia toward a more aloof position vis-à-vis the Western alliance; is preoccupied with regions and countries along Russia's immediate periphery; and is prone to outbursts of great-power assertiveness in seeking to rebuild Russia's sphere of influence. At best it is a consensus regarding Russia's special responsibility in the Commonwealth of Independent States. At worst it is a consensus about its special right in the former Soviet Union as its presumed exclusive sphere of influence.

Far from resurrecting the old Soviet Union, Moscow's new quest for a sphere of influence and attempts to articulate its own "Monroe Doctrine" represent a search for a new identity and strategic posture. Russian aspiration to play the role of the sole arbiter and enforcer of security and stability throughout the former Soviet Union is counterbalanced by a deeply rooted and persisting realization that the cost of a sphere of influence, let alone a full-scale empire, would put a severe burden on the already strained Russian treasury. Moscow's newly found rhetorical assertiveness in the area of foreign policy and relations with the "near abroad" is more likely to be a long-run indicator of some of the underlying objectives of Russian foreign policy than the basis for short-term predictions about and assessments of Russian actions.

This direction of Russian foreign policy is the result of the domestic political and economic transformation of Russia in the first two years following the breakup of the Soviet Union. The shock of early post-Soviet reforms, which were closely identified with the pro-Western course of the Gaydar cabinet, has produced a significant degree of disillusionment with the West and the United States, as well as with the course of close partnership with Washington. The depth of Russia's economic decline and the long road to recovery would, in the eyes of many Russians, effectively preclude Moscow's participation in that partnership as an equal. Hence, Russia would have to pursue its own independent course in foreign and security policy commensurate with its means and consistent with its great-power aspirations. The gradual replacement of Western-oriented "market romantics" in Moscow's policymaking arena with "pragmatists" who identify more closely with large state interests has been accompanied by a change in rhetoric that has come to emphasize relations with the "near abroad" and integration of the post-Soviet states as key goals of Russian foreign policy.

The new foreign and security policy consensus has been reflected in the deliberations of individual analysts and of private think tanks, as well as in institutional positions of the key players in the seemingly erratic and ill-organized Russian policy process. The Ministry of Foreign Affairs, under the leadership of Andrey Kozyrev (once thought to be the successor to Shevardnadze and the pillar of Russia's Western-oriented foreign policy), has pursued a tough rhetorical line on the "near abroad" and become a staunch defender of Russia's much-debated national interests.

Russia's military establishment, already marred by allegations of widespread meddling in various regional conflicts in the former Soviet Union, has embraced the notion that the "near abroad" will forever remain the sphere of vital interest and exclusive influence of Russia. The refocusing of the Russian military's attention on the "near abroad" has been amply demonstrated in the new doctrine adopted in 1993.

This picture of institutional consensus is complemented by the legislative branch—the Duma. The presence of large statist—communist, agrarian, nationalist, and industrialist—interests virtually guarantees that the new legislature will not engage in aggressive pursuit of a pro-Western foreign and security policy course any more than the last one did, and that its efforts will be devoted to the task of defining and protecting Russian interests in the "near abroad."

The emerging foreign and security policy consensus has been demonstrated in Moscow's reaction to the two critical Western policy initiatives—expansion of NATO and PFP. Whereas the former was deemed downright harmful to Russian interests, the latter received a lukewarm welcome that holds out the promise of a reluctant minimal participation at best, rather than a true partnership.

Pragmatism, realism, and gradualism have emerged as key themes of the new Russian consensus in the area of national security and foreign policy. Driven by a combination of domestic political factors, a degree of disappointment with early post-Soviet "romanticism," reaction to the West's own policy toward Russia, and a genuine, objective desire to chart the long-term strategic direction for Russian foreign and security policies, the emphasis on pragmatism, realism, and gradualism should not be prejudged as a sign of Russian irredentism. A certain degree of recoiling from the "romantic" phase was inevitable, as Russia proceeds on its quest for a place in the international system without the Soviet Union and undergoes a profound ideological transformation.

Russia's quest for a lasting vision of national interest and a place in the international arena without the Soviet Union poses a number of difficult questions for U.S. policymakers; the answers are likely to have far-reaching implications for U.S. post–cold war policy, not only toward the former Soviet Union but toward other regions of the world as well.

A key issue in this context is the contradiction between U.S. recognition of sovereignty, independence, and territorial integrity of the newly independent states around Russia's periphery on the one hand, and Russian aspirations for a special role in the "post-Soviet space" on the other. U.S. interest in maintaining good relations with Russia could come into conflict with the Russian claim to a *droit de regard* over the newly independent states. In the view of this author, under the best of circumstances, Russia could and should play the role of the pillar of security and stability in the former Soviet Union. Under a far less optimistic and perhaps more realistic scenario, Russian pursuit of national interest would impinge on the sovereignty and independence of some of its neighbors.

Moreover, in certain circumstances, such as general political instability and inter-ethnic conflict, Russian interests in its former colonies may warrant (from Moscow's point of view) intervention in the "near abroad." More likely than not, such intervention will occur against the will of local governments. Having recognized the independence and sovereignty of the former Soviet republics, the United States would have to choose between confronting Russia and condoning its aggression.

U.S. policymakers would face the task of balancing the right to sovereignty, self-determination, and territorial integrity of the newly independent states against the need to restore stability and order in a given region, as well as the desire to sustain continuity in U.S.–Russian relations. Recognizing the tension between the obligations of international law and the realistic limitations on U.S. foreign policy, one has little choice but to acknowledge that our commitment to furthering the principles of self-determination, sovereignty, and territorial integrity will have to be constrained by practical concerns for prevention of conflict and loss of life. In the view of this author, such considerations must take precedence over the principles of sovereignty and territorial integrity, as well as the desire for self-determination. Although little can be done after the fact, it is also important to recognize, with a view toward future contingencies, that in some instances recognition of the newly independent states in recent years may have been premature.

Moscow may find itself not fully in control of events and pushed along the interventionist path in the adjacent Russophone provinces by domestic political pressures to protect compatriots abroad. The contagion of separatism may well spread from Ukraine to Kazakhstan's Northern provinces, for example, embroiling Russia in conflict whether it likes it or not, pushing it toward the path of reexpansion and undoing the Commonwealth of Independent States.

Ironically, a major concern for Western policymakers under such grim circumstances could be not to protect the newly independent states from Russian neoimperialism, but to help Russia steer clear of its postimperial burden.

No easy recipes are available to Western or Russian policymakers to correct the existing situation or to avert future dramatic contingencies. Even formal recognition (however difficult it would prove to codify) of Russia's special role throughout the former Soviet Union still begs the question of Russia's ability to play that role. At the same time, it is important for the international community to recognize that Russia does play a special role in that sphere and that it has special interests there. To do otherwise would be unrealistic, unfair, and unwise.

Admittedly, the Western community has little leverage over Russian policies, both real and declaratory, toward the former Soviet Union. But it can play a constructive role, albeit remaining largely on the margins. Stabilization through economic assistance to the "lesser equals" in the CIS will prove beneficial to Russia's own interests. Perhaps, given Russia's own uncertain path regarding its neighbors, the best that the West can do is to help create a more stable environment around it.